LICENSED TO LIVE

LICENSED TO LIVE

Daily Affirmations to Rebuild Your Life

Jarret "Doctor Jarret" Patton, MD, FAAP

LICENSED TO LIVE:
DAILY AFFIRMATIONS TO REBUILD YOUR LIFE

Published by Purposely Created Publishing Group™

Printed in the United States of America

ISBN: 978-1-64484-228-7

Special discounts are available on bulk quantity purchases by book clubs, associations and special interest groups. For details email: sales@publishyourgift.com or call (888) 949-6228.

For information logon to: www.PublishYourGift.com

*This book is dedicated to my parents,
Paulette and Roy, who instilled the power of
positive thinking into me at a young age.*

INTRODUCTION

After I wrote my award-winning book *Licensed to Live: A Primer to Rebuilding Your Life After Your Career is Shattered*, I caught the author bug. This particular book is a bit different than the others in that the goal is to help you focus on your positive thinking. Throughout the struggles outlined in *Licensed to Live*, there were a lot of things that helped me get through "the storm" and bounce back to attain even higher (and unimaginable to myself) heights. My faith, my family, and daily exercise helped to get me through. However, the power of positive thinking is something that I strongly believe in AND practice. It made a huge difference during my greatest comeback. Take a few minutes to learn how to use your affirmations and then get started with day one!

Using Affirmations Effectively

One of the top questions people ask is, "How often should I say my affirmations?" The answer varies. The short answer is at least three times a day and as much as you need. Just as you customize the phrasing of affirmations to meet your needs, customize the frequency and timing, as well.

Another question people ask is, "How quickly will I see results?" This probably isn't what you want to hear but, realistically, the time frame is different for each person and depends on multiple factors, which are specific to you.

For many people, the emphasis is on the "quick" part. Think about how long it took for your thought patterns and habits to develop to their current state. If you're most interested in how fast you can change something, you might need to begin by changing your mindset and priorities.

Focus on making steady progress towards your goal, first and foremost. This is not about how fast you get there, but how long you stay once you reach your destination. Perseverance and staying power will help you to achieve and maintain the changes over the long-term. Developing these qualities as you make progress is important to your overall success and happiness.

With that in mind, implementing a few creative techniques, activities, and ideas can add an element of fun, making the entire experience more beneficial. Let's look at how to use affirmations effectively and have fun as you make breakthrough after breakthrough.

Powerful Practices for Rewarding Results

Sometimes, reaching your goals and making permanent changes can be difficult. Using positive affirmations as part of your strategy can play a big part in your success. However, positive affirmations are not a stand-alone solution. Saying or thinking positive words will only get you so far.

Consider the person who wants to lose weight. That person might use the positive affirmation, "I am losing weight." Affirmations are not magic words that make things happen. While there is power in words, the real power is within you; it is in your thoughts, words, and actions. It takes all three of these things to reach your realistic goals.

For example, in addition to saying, "I am losing weight," the person who wants to lose weight must do things such as change their eating and exercise habits. Achieving your goal requires that you take actions to change, as well as reminding yourself that you can and are making changes. This is where using your positive affirmations effectively comes into play.

Affirmation/Statement Types

Essentially, affirmations are statements said with confidence about a perceived truth. In this book, the terms affirmations and statements are often interchangeable. However, when referring to the positive statements used to help you make changes, the term affirmation(s) is used and preferred.

Affirmations can be either negative or positive. Let's begin with negative statements and affirmations first, because they may block or limit your successes without you even realizing it. The more you understand about negative statements, the easier it will be to identify, counteract, and overcome them with positive belief statements or affirmations, and other tools.

Negative Statements

You have experienced positive and negative affirmations. In fact, you may vividly remember a negative statement that hurt your feelings or made you feel bad about yourself. This is the case with most negative statements. They tend to include negative words such as don't, won't, am not, can't, shouldn't, and never, among others.

With a negative statement, you probably feel a strong emotion such as fear, anger, pain, sadness, worthlessness, etc. Even when a statement is inaccurate or untrue, a part of you still remembers how it made (or still makes) you feel and automatically accepts the statement as being true or possible, on some level.

Because strong emotions are linked to negative statements, the memories and effects are likely to stick with you and nullify or override positive statements. As an adult, you may discover that negative statements made during your childhood still affect how you see yourself and others.

Positive Statements

No matter what part of your life you want to change, positive affirmations can help you achieve your goals. However, there are no quick fixes, so don't expect any. Changing your thoughts, beliefs, habits, and parts of your life take time. If something is deeply ingrained, it may take longer and more effort to achieve your goal. But positive affirmations can support and enhance your progress from the first day by helping you…

- Develop a positive outlook
- Broaden your opportunities
- Counteract negative statements
- Focus on and achieve healthy goals
- Increase your confidence
- See yourself as a beautiful person
- Change unhealthy behaviors
- Take control of your life
- Respect and love yourself
- Modify your thought patterns
- Persevere to make progress
- Motivate yourself to take action, and so much more

Let's get started!

You know that you can write your positive affirmations down and use them in your self-talk; but, let's face it, this can get a little boring after a while and you may find that you aren't as excited as you once were about your affirmations. To help you stay motivated, interested, positive, and on course, this book was written with space to write down other thoughts or complete an exercise that will go along with your affirmation. To get the most out of your investment, take the time to read, write, and make your affirmation actionable. Let's get started today with day one.

1.

I see problems as interesting challenges.

Problems often distract us or serve as roadblocks. Write down one or two problems that you will take on as a challenge and turn into an opportunity.

2.

I am bold and courageous.

Fear often holds us back or limits our results. Write down one bold and courageous action that you will take today to break free of something that fear has kept you from doing.

3.

I let go of worries and
replace them with
excitement and optimism.

Stop worrying and let it go. Write down one thing that worried you when you awoke today and resolve to let it go. Your future is bright.

4.

I brighten another person's day by doing something with them.

You are a person of many talents. Write down one talent that you will share with others today.

5.

I make decisions that always lead to something positive, in time.

Decisions you make today have positive consequences at some point in the future. Write down one decision that you thought was bad at the time that yielded positive results.

6.

I practice my skills each day to attain greatness.

At times, we take our skills for granted. Write down one skill you will practice today.

7.

I breathe in calmness and
breathe out nervousness.

Take two minutes to inhale calmness and exhale nervousness.

8.

This situation works out
for my highest good.

The situation you are facing will work out. Write a map of the steps you will take to go from tragedy to triumph.

9.

I forgive myself for things
I have done in the past.

You can't change your past but you can shape your future. Forgive yourself of something in your past so that you can focus on your future.

10.

I let go of my anger so
that I can see clearly.

Anger clouds your vision. Get a clearer view by writing down one thing that you will not be angry about any more.

11.

I receive all feedback
with appreciation.

Feedback is designed to improve you as a leader. Write down one piece of feedback you received that you didn't take to heart and why.

12.

All that I need comes to me
at the right time and place.

Patience is a virtue. Write down one thing you don't have in life that you are willing to wait for.

13.

I develop the mindset to praise myself.

Praise yourself today for something that you did yesterday and make sure you praise yourself for something you do today, and tomorrow.

14.

I love meeting new people and approach them with confidence and interest.

We have the opportunity to meet new people every day. Identify one failed opportunity to meet a new person yesterday and resolve to meet someone new today. Write down where you intend to meet this person.

15.

I attract positive, confident people
because I am one of them.

You are a combination of the five people you spend the most time with. Write down five positive and confident people you wish to spend more time with.

16.

I fill my mind with positive,
nourishing thoughts.

Write down one or two negative thoughts and strike a line through them. Replace them with one or two positive thoughts that you will carry through the rest of your day.

17.

My life, experiences, beliefs, and actions inspire and benefit others.

Your collective experiences will help someone today. Write down one person that you intend to help today and when you will help them.

18.

I see myself as a gift to people in my community and nation.

Volunteering your time, gifts, and talents in your community uplifts everyone. Write down one charitable action you intend to accomplish during the next 72 days that you will perform.

19.

There is an important reason
that this is unfolding now.

There is opportunity in every action and every distraction. Write down something that is unfolding in front of you now and how it becomes an opportunity for your future good.

20.

I ask my loved ones to support my efforts.

There are times when our loved ones don't seem to support our efforts. Call one person today and help them understand why you need their support.

21.

I accept everyone as they are and continue to pursue my dreams.

Think of one person that you will accept as they are and write down how accepting that person will help you achieve your dreams (not distract you from them).

22.

I have long-lasting friendships because I accept others, unconditionally.

Write down five longtime friends that you accept unconditionally or write down the names of two that you will accept going forward.

23.

I attract positive people who become life-long friends.

Keep the positivity going. Write down the name of a friend you want to become more positive and how you will help them accomplish this task.

24.

I surround myself with
people who treat me well.

If someone doesn't treat you well, step away and move on. Write down the initials of a person that you need to walk away from and forgive them for their actions.

25.

When I breathe, I inhale confidence and exhale doubt.

Take two minutes to breathe in confidence and breathe out doubt.

26.

I take the time to show my friends that I care about them.

Call or write someone who you haven't connected with recently and let them know that you care.

27.

My friends do not judge me.

Write down the name of a person that you will no longer judge.

28.

I take comfort in the fact that
I can always leave a situation.

You are the ultimate decision maker. Think of a situation that you are willing to walk away from if things don't turn around in the next 14 days. Write down the date 14 days from now.

29.

It is easy for me to look in the mirror and say, “I love you.”

Every time you look in a mirror today, say, “I love you.”

30.

I receive kindness and love multiple times a day.

Write down an instance in which a total stranger showed you kindness and love this week and have gratitude.

31.

I live in the present and am confident of the future.

Let go of one thing from your past and write down one positive thing you see coming in your future.

32.

I am surrounded by abundance.

Your mind can trick you into thinking the universe is limited. But, you are surrounded by abundance as the universe is unlimited. Take a moment to reflect and embrace abundance.

33.

I attract money effortlessly and easily.

Remind yourself of a time when money just appeared. It will come again.

34.

I continuously discover
new avenues of income.

Don't limit yourself to one source of income. Write down three new ways that you can earn money.

35.

I am open to all the wealth
life has to offer.

Wealth is not only about money. Write down several ways in which you are wealthy.

36.

I use money to better other people's lives.

Spread your money around. List one charitable cash contribution that you will make this week.

37.

I am a better person because of my hardships and achievements.

Celebrate a win you had yesterday that resulted from a previous hardship.

38.

I deserve abundance
and prosperity.

You work hard. You deserve a lot of things. Write down your next scheduled vacation. If you don't have one, plan it.

39.

I manage my money wisely.

List three ways that you could manage your money better.

40.

I am sometimes meant to deliver a gift or blessing rather than keep it.

Pass it forward. Think of a time when someone gave you a gift. When will you pass a gift on to someone else?

41.

I am destined to find prosperity
in everything I do.

If you don't believe it who will?

42.

I am thankful for the abundance I have in my life.

Spend three minutes writing a gratitude list.

43.

I rejoice for others who are prosperous and share the abundance.

Be joyous for others when they succeed. There is enough for everyone. If there was someone that had a recent success and you did not congratulate them, do that today.

44.

Today is the future I created yesterday. Tomorrow will be even better!

There is no time to dwell in the past. Write down one thing today that will make your tomorrow better and do it.

45.

I am healthy, energetic,
and optimistic.

Even when we are not at our best, we must train our minds to believe that we are. List one thing you can do to improve your health today. List one thing you can do to give yourself more energy today. Find one thing to be optimistic about today.

46.

I exercise regularly to strengthen my body.

We don't always get the exercise that we want or need. Make a commitment to exercise today for at least 10 minutes. If you have already exercised today, write down your exercise plan for the week.

47.

I enjoy exercising and
strengthening my muscles.

You may not like exercising all the time. However, your mind and body need it. Write down one physical activity that you enjoy and commit to doing it in the next 48 hours.

48.

My body is healing, and
I feel better every day.

Your health may not be where you want it to be, but know that your body is healing every day. List one thing you will do today to make yourself feel better tomorrow.

49.

I release stress from my body with every exhaled breath.

Spend two minutes breathing out stress.

50.

I pay attention to what my body needs for health and vitality.

Listen to your body. Write down one thing your body needs today that you haven't given to it. What are you waiting for? Give it today.

51.

I sleep soundly and peacefully.

There are many things that you can do to improve your sleep. Go to sleep tonight thankful for all the blessings that came to you during the day. List a few of those blessings.

52.

I am surrounded by people who encourage and support healthy choices.

Commit to adding someone to your list that fits within this category.

53.

My body, mind, and soul work together efficiently to keep me healthy.

You must exercise all three. How will you exercise each today?

54.

I stay up to date about
my health issues.

If you aren't, make a call today. If you are, make one healthier choice today.

55.

I am very grateful I am
at this weight.

This is one that many of us are not happy with; however, things could be worse. Spend three minutes showing gratitude for the health that you do have.

56.

I appreciate every cell in my body.

You are already a trillionaire; you have trillions of cells in your body. Spend three minutes showing gratitude for every cell in your body, from the bottom of your feet to the top of your head.

57.

I am filled with excitement
when I look in the mirror.

Say, “I love you” each time you look in the mirror today. Write “I love you” below.

58.

Everything I think, say, and do makes me healthier.

Write down one thing you are thinking right now and how that makes you healthier.

59.

My job adds satisfaction and fulfillment to my life.

Think carefully about this one. If your job is not a positive force in your life, it is time to refresh or restart. Make a list of things that would make your job better. Use this list to start a conversation with your boss.

60.

My career provides me the right opportunities to grow.

Your career should utilize many of your gifts and talents. Make a list of ways you can grow in your current job.

61.

I play a big role in my own career success.

You are responsible for your success. How will you become more successful in your career?

62.

My work (business) makes a profound difference in this world.

If you are not making a difference, you are not doing the right thing. List one thing that you made a difference in yesterday. List one thing that you will do today to make a difference.

63.

I am a better businessperson because of my mistakes.

Be grateful for your mistakes as they are learning opportunities. Think of a recent time that you made a mistake and what you learned from it.

64.

I breathe deeply, exercise regularly, and feed my body nutritious food.

Do all three things today. No excuses.

65.

I have my dream job.

There are times when you need help to get to your dream job. Where will you go for help to make your job a dream?

66.

I love every day that I work.

Be grateful that you work, enjoy every day. Write down one thing that brings you joy in your job daily.

67.

My job brings me
financial abundance.

Although it might be nice to have more, take a moment to be grateful for what your job has provided.

68.

My coworkers love being around me.

You bring so much to the table. List five reasons why your coworkers love you.

69.

My boss values the work I do.

You may not hear it every day; but, a smart boss values your contributions. Make a list of the things that you do to bring value to your job.

70.

My positive attitude, confidence, and good work attracts new opportunities.

Think of a recent time an opportunity presented itself because of your hard work, positive attitude, and confidence. What will be your next opportunity?

71.

I am enthusiastic and excited about my work.

The more you are excited, the more others around you become excited. What are you excited about today?

72.

My enthusiasm about my job is contagious.

How has your attitude towards your job affected others?

73.

I speak positively about my coworkers.

A positive attitude can shape the environment in which you work. Think of the last time you spoke positively about your coworkers. What positive thing(s) will you say to your coworkers the next time you see them?

74.

I find optimistic ways of dealing with difficulties.

Difficulties are problems that need a solution. List one difficulty in your life and propose three different optimistic solutions to the problem.

75.

I find the best solutions to problems by listening and learning from others.

Problems are not unique to the individual. Who will you listen to and learn from to help solve your problems?

76.

I look at things from multiple perspectives to see the big picture.

There are so many different ways to solve a problem. Think of a problem you face now and look at it from at least five points of view to help clarify the big picture.

77.

I take a mini break from
the problem to let my
subconscious find the answer.

Get freedom from your problem by not giving it your conscious attention today. Let your subconscious mind do the work. Write the problem below and don't think about it again today.

78.

I seek out a new way of thinking about this situation.

Who will you enlist to help you think about this situation? Sometimes a little help is all you need.

79.

I release my need to have
the approval of others.

Your biggest fan should be yourself as others don't affect your ability to achieve. Give yourself a pat on the back and write something you are proud about below.

80.

I'm excited about the amazing people I will meet today.

You are supposed to meet the people placed onto your path. Write down where you will meet someone new today.

81.

I choose to free myself
from all negativity that
hampers my progress.

Happiness is a choice. Negativity is a choice. Positivity is a choice. Make a list of the negative forces in your life (on a separate piece of paper) and put it in the shredder (or rip the paper to shreds) to free yourself from the negativity.

82.

I press on because I believe my path will prepare me for success.

There are many distractions in life. These distractions are only detours. Look back at your path and write down one instance in which a detour in your path prepared you for future success.

83.

I use strategies that motivate me to move forward.

Investment in yourself will help improve you and others around you. What are you willing to invest in order to move yourself forward?

84.

I make a conscious choice to be happy.

What is your choice today? Do you choose to be happy or sad? Write that choice below.

85.

I look at the world around
me and I can't help but
to smile and feel joy.

There is joy in everything. Sometimes you have to look for it. Why do you feel like smiling and having joy in this exact moment?

86.

I am grateful for this moment
which enriches my life.

Fill this page with things you are grateful for.

87.

I accept and embrace all experiences, even unpleasant ones.

Even the unpleasant experiences are made to strengthen you and prepare you for greatness. List a couple of unpleasant experiences and how they have helped or will help you achieve greatness.

88.

I believe in my ability to find and navigate the path that's right for me.

Although you may have become lost along the way, uncertainty is only temporary. Be certain that you will find the right path. List three resources that you can use to get back on the right track.

89.

I release the past and live fully in the present moment.

Holding on to the past is one way to certainly slow down your progress. Accept the past as you can't change it. Write down a thought you have in this present moment and how it will shape your future.

90.

I inhale deeply and let peace and happiness fill my mind and body.

Take three minutes to breathe in peace and happiness then write down how you feel. Remember happiness is a choice.

EPILOGUE

Thank you for purchasing this book. I hope that it helped you move forward in your positive outlook on your career and life. Positive thinking is one tool to keep you moving towards your goals and objectives. However, it takes more than just positive thoughts to turn your dreams into reality. Make sure you are taking action towards your goals every day.

Congratulations! By now you should observe the transformation of your powerfully positive thought patterns. After these 90 days, you should notice the change in your thoughts and your speech when talking about yourself and others. You should celebrate the changes that you are making! Feel free to start this book over again from day one and you will see how your mind has changed. For an additional challenge to keep your momentum, consider writing your own daily positive affirmations.

Sometimes you may need a little help or guidance to get where you ultimately want to be. Don't be afraid to continue to invest in yourself. After all, you are your most valuable asset in life and business (whether your own or someone else's). If you feel the positive change and want to know where to go from here, don't hesitate to reach out to me through my website: www.doctorjarret.com

CPSIA information can be obtained
at www.ICGtesting.com
Printed in the USA
BVHW042355300720
585040BV00005B/342